To those who have seen the Child,
however dimly,
however incredulously,
the TIME BEING is,
in a sense,
the most trying time of all.

W. H. Auden

Layout: Marilyn Guerdan

PRAYERS
for the time being

Max Pauli, C.SS.R.

Drawings by Sister Claret, SSND

Liguori Publications
Liguori, Missouri 63057

Imprimi Potest:
Daniel L. Lowery, C.SS.R.
Provincial, St. Louis Province
Redemptorist Fathers
August 30, 1971

Imprimatur:
St. Louis, September 2, 1971
+ John J. Cardinal Carberry
Archbishop of St. Louis

IN THE FEWEST WORDS

If I knew what prayer was,
I would certainly be willing to tell you,
but all I know is when it happens.
It happens when I become self-aware
of my happiness, needs, anger, pity,
of any feeling storming my tired heart,
and when, at the same time,
I become aware that God is here too,
the eternal listener
so concerned with me and everyone
that He stoops down from His eternity
to hear our meager self-reflections.
I know for certain that I prayed once
when an old cat was entering into labor;
once, when I was alone on the highway
blown along by a romping blizzard;
once, when I was shocked to hear
a friend had drowned in the green sea.
I prayed because I was aware
of something stirring in my soul,
demanding an expression to Someone
who was bigger, wiser, stronger
than I could ever be on my own.
If this is any use to you, take it,
because the heart of prayer is sharing.

Max Pauli, C.SS.R.

for my parents
who gave me the stability
of love
and
for John Duffy, C.SS.R.,
who showed me the way
to the mountain
and provided reasons
for coming back

TABLE OF CONTENTS

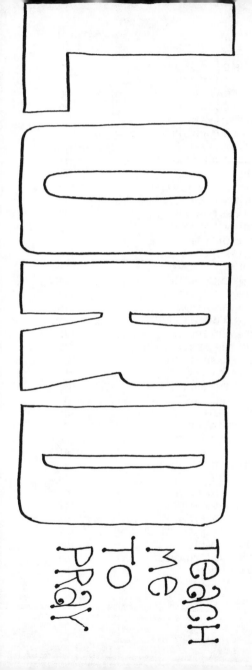

LORD
Teach Me To Pray

1. PRAYER ON PRAYER

I'm no good, Lord,
at praying to You at all.
Compared to Your saints
who raised gothic cathedrals of prayer,
what can I build
except sand castles, maybe,
because that's the kind of person I am?
After all, what can I pray about?
I've never had a Dark Night of the Soul,
or felt a crisis of faith,
or been caught short in ecstasy.
My prayers
would have to be about engine knock,
or my war with red roaches,
or the size I hope to be after my diet.
I'm really afraid
my prayers will bore You to death,
and yet I do want to share
my midget miseries
and skinny successes with You.
Later on, Lord,
I may invent more fantastic prayers,
but right now I'm in the time being,
and this will have to do.
Amen.

2. PRAYER FOR A RAINY DAY

Today is a wet day, Lord,
with the rain slanting down
like so many silver strings from heaven.
Later on I have to go outside
when I'll probably get drenched
and feel soggy for hours,
but right now I'm inside
where it's dry and quiet,
so let me thank You for the rain
before I happen to forget.
I like Your rain for many reasons:
it soothes my battered nerves,
it washes down the sooty streets,
it makes our garage roof
beat with furious drumming.
But I specially like Your rain
because it makes things grow.
It reaches down into the earth
with its tiny fingers
and taps the seeds awake.
It says to them —
"Time to get up, time to sprout,
time to make things green and lovely."
Lord, I know this sounds silly,
but let me be like the rain.

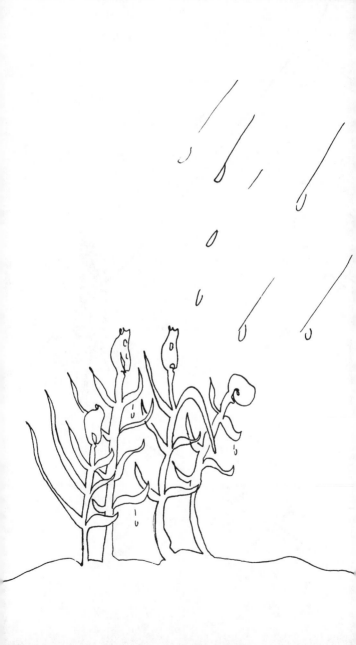

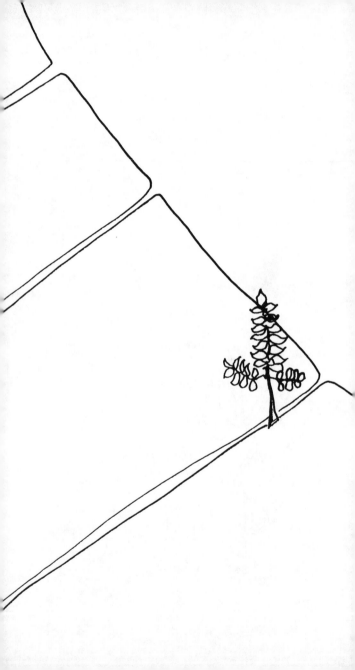

3. PRAYER ON A PLUM PIT

This spring, Lord, I found a plum pit
lodged in a crack in my pavement,
and do You know,
it was sprouting tiny roots
as thin as thread,
and throwing out a cluster of leaves
no larger than a match tip?
I don't know why,
but I dug it up
and then planted it tenderly
in an old pot filled with loam.
Through all the summer I studied it,
stretching itself upward toward the sun
which gleamed like jade
on its chlorophyll branches.
Each morning I'd water it
with a mixture of plant food,
and then count the leaves
to see if it had invented a new one.
Even now when I approach it,
I still feel strange, Lord,
almost in awe with being this close
to something mysterious as life itself,
even in such a quiet form
as a plum pit.

4. PRAYER FOR A FIRST CHILD

Now that it's over, Lord, thank You,
because both my wife and my little boy
are doing just fine.
I've even seen him already,
in one of those incubators,
red and wrinkled
and, to me, totally beautiful.
You wouldn't think something that small
could be alive,
but he is,
shaking his midget fists at the world
and screaming:
Look out, I'm here.

He is here, Lord, all here,
yet the world won't look out,
and he won't have that glass hothouse
to protect him like a rose.
He'll have to grow up,
and be stepped on,
and stand alone against the rain of knocks
the world is always too ready to provide.
So be with him, Lord, as I will,
at least long enough
to see his own image made over
in the joy of a first child.

5. A HOUSEWIFE'S PRAYER

I was up early again this morning, Lord,
clearing away last night's debris,
so now I'm a little tired.
It seems I lack the endurance I once had
when I could breeze through a day
and not feel exhausted by night.
So, Lord, I'm asking You
to give me strength because I need it,
not just for myself alone,
but for those I love and serve.
I need strength
to be patient with the children
who still have unbounded energy
for making noise and breaking things;
I need strength
to take a keen interest
in the affairs that interest my husband;
I need strength
to bear with the aches of my parents
who are growing so old.
I need strength
to carry my little household crosses
as You carried Your great one.
And, in case I forgot to mention it,
thank You for listening to me, Lord.

6. A FATHER'S PRAYER

Well, Lord, it's another day
and I must force myself out
to scrabble for another dollar,
but a dollar doesn't go far any more.
Sometimes, when things crowd together,
I get so disgusted with life —
with wars that don't make sense,
with competing against people I like,
with the lack of certainty
that keeps me on edge all the time.
So, Lord, I ask You to help me
in making life different somehow,
so I can entrust a better world
into the hands of my children,
a world full of honor and trust,
where every face is brightly stamped
with Your obvious image.
Still, if I can't be a great success
in changing the shape of the world,
at least let me be a small success
in changing the shape of my own life,
making me into the father
that my children so much deserve.
This is all I have to say, Lord,
but I ask Your help anyway.

7. PRAYER ON KINDERGARTEN

Well, there he goes, Lord,
the brave soldier marching off to war,
except that in this case
the soldier is just five years old,
and war is only his first day at school.
Right now, I feel nothing but euphoria
to know that some other heroic soul
has taken the duty on her shoulders
of picking up after him,
of refereeing his many fights,
of teaching him the basics of manners.
But the more I think about it,
the more a different feeling
begins to cloud slowly over my heart;
and it is that he no longer needs me,
he is beginning to stand on his own.
There I go, Lord, branding myself
as a typical ambivalent mother
who wants her children to be independent
while yet wanting them to depend on her.
I know I've fought my possessiveness,
and tried to give them boulder strength
instead of a trellis for clinging vines.
But, Lord, he's only five years old:
does he have to be a rock so soon?

8. PRAYER FOR MONDAYS

When the alarm rang this morning, Lord,
I thought I must have set it wrong
because it just couldn't have been
rising time already.
But it was.
And when I pulled back the curtain
and looked out sleepily,
it seemed to me
as if someone had painted the world
in varied shades of gray.
I should have known though,
because Mondays are always like that:
days of dragging my tired body around,
of running out of life's necessities
like cigarettes and coffee,
of having the sink plug up,
or vacuum cleaner short out,
or washer die in the middle of a load.
Who invented Mondays anyway?
Yet I suppose I'll survive
and be my bright bubbling self
when the kids scream in from school,
and my husband parks our dented car.
So, Lord, just give me a little support
to get from now to then.

9. PRAYER ON A YOUNG GIRL

Well, Lord, at last it's started,
now that my daughter has discovered
there's more to boys than baseball.
In a way,
she's rather cute about the process,
washing her hair nightly and setting it,
complaining about her many freckles,
trying on less exotic shades of make-up
while hoping I don't notice.
Yet it disturbs me too, Lord,
because at this age
she's so vulnerable to male attention,
so easily crushed,
so easily led on.
And what can I do?
Restrictions and motherly advice
will seem medieval to her modern notions,
but I must protect her
·like the picket fence
around the young rosebush
until she is ready to stand alone.
So, Lord,
without failing by repressive love
or boneless laxity,
help me to help her grow.

10. PRAYER ON DATING

I have a boy friend, Lord,
who tends to think of necking
as the world's only year-round sport.
Outside of that, he's fine:
responsible in his job,
honest to his parents,
idealistic in everything
but his attitude toward sex.
In fact, he as much as said
you'll never know what you can get
until first you've tried to get it.
He swears that he loves me,
and thinks of me in terms of marriage,
but, Lord,
his assets seem so shallow
when he can't respect my feelings.
What complicates the issue
is that I think I love him too,
and can sense myself wavering
between my beliefs and his.
So, Lord, be with me on our next date,
because it's either a draw
between his convictions and mine,
or one of us will win out,
and You alone know which.

11. PRAYER ON NEIGHBORS

Lately, Lord,
I've been sympathizing with goldfish,
because I know how they must feel,
being stared at constantly
in their glass houses.
Well, my home isn't all glass,
but it does have enough doors and windows
to make it a good facsimile,
and my neighbors do treat me
like some private pet,
always peering over the fence,
or watching from their kitchen,
as I go about my housework.
We've been living next to each other
for a good many years,
so you'd think
they'd have grown tired of my routine,
the day-in and day-out sameness,
but it seems otherwise.
Yet it doesn't anger me any more, Lord,
to be the subject of their spying,
but only sad,
to realize
they have so little life to live
that they must be always watching mine.

12. PRAYER ON BEAUTY

Well, Lord, what happens now
when I have to face up to being plain?
For as long as I can remember
I've been waiting for that magic moment
when suddenly it would hit me
that I was beautiful,
that my dull hair was dazzling,
my cloudy eyes radiant,
my pinched smile devastating.
Well, I've had enough of waiting, Lord,
because You've been no fairy godmother
to this modern Cinderella.
I suppose I should be thankful
for the hidden assets You've given me,
but I've already brainwashed myself
into neglecting them as unimportant
while I read the latest beauty hints,
listened to the luring voice of glamour
whispering constantly in my ear,
and prayed to You for the miracle.
All right, Lord, I get the point
that I should start developing
my other gifts as compensation,
but at least give me time
to adapt to being just plain me.

13. PRAYER ON SEX

Lord, You gave me my sex,
but it's a gift
that confuses me altogether.
I know well enough
that You intended it
to be a special thing set apart,
but sometimes my hunger gets so strong
that it almost drives me
over the brink of decency.
I have this fear, Lord,
that I won't be able to manage it alone,
that I'll transform it
into something warped and ugly,
when it should be my unique response
to Your creative act.
So I'm asking You for help
before I explode:
help in fathoming the mystery of sex,
help in facing up to it
as a human being with dignity,
and help in controlling it
before I go off the deep end.
Lord, if You who made me
don't give me help,
then there is no one left to turn to.

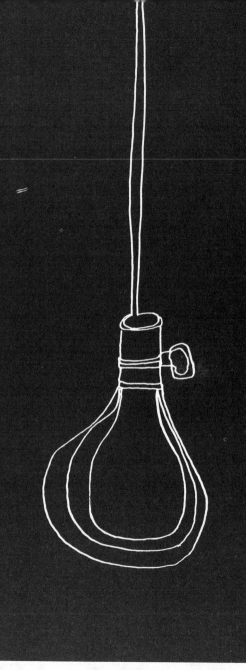

14. PRAYER FOR SLEEPLESS NIGHTS

Two nights ago, Lord,
it was the amorous cat next door;
then, last night,
the impatient scream of an ambulance;
and now, tonight,
it's some neighborhood dog
howling its lungs out at the moon.
I'm beginning to wonder, Lord,
if I'll ever get a full night's sleep.
Even wondering about it
is enough to keep me awake,
listening to my clock's tick-ticking
as it inches toward the hour of the bell.
I need my sleep, Lord:
I need it to keep me human,
because without it I'm only a machine
for making assorted grumpy noises,
and not even a well-wound one at that.
So, Lord, help me
to get a good night's sleep,
a sleep that knits me together
and prepares me for the job at hand.
It's not an important job,
but it's mine,
so let me rest up to do it adequately.

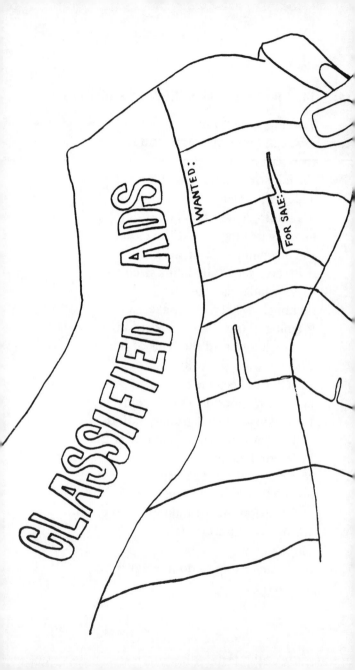

15. PRAYER FOR JOB HUNTERS

For weeks, Lord, I've made a ritual
of scanning the morning papers
for want ads on work;
I've walked up countless stairs,
and spent innumerable hours
waiting for interviews in drab offices;
I've made so many phone calls of inquiry
that my mother's bill
will probably approximate
the cash worth of Fort Knox.
But still, nothing.
Either I'm too young,
or too inexperienced,
or just too plain late.
Obviously, I'm frustrated, Lord,
but I can't dare allow myself
the luxury of giving up the search,
because that would again throw me
upon the good will of my parents,
who are too generous already.
I know there must be some job
that I can fill, Lord,
if only You will grant me the grace
of allowing it and my tired self
to come in contact.

16. A WAITRESS' PRAYER

Being a waitress
is only a temporary job for me, Lord,
while I look for something better,
but still
this meanwhile routine depresses me:
not so much the walking,
and the carrying of trays,
and the pouring of coffee,
and the cleaning off of tables,
but rather the business of smiling
at the nasty quirks of diners.
True, the customer is always right,
but daily it is getting more difficult
to live up to that grand motto,
especially with some people
who send food back as inedible,
or insult the service,
or imagine alien particles in the soup.
Sometimes I reach the edge of explosion
when it demands a supreme effort
not to let them have
a waitress' point of view on good manners.
If nothing else, Lord,
I've learned what I must have acted like
before I got this present job.

17. PRAYER ON HOMESICKNESS

This is the first time
I've ever been away from home, Lord,
and each mile the bus grinds off
makes me feel more miserable and alone.
It all began when I climbed aboard
and saw my parents on the platform
waving their last good-bys,
and it suddenly struck me
how this was my decision to leave.
I wanted to take back that choice,
give up the possibility of a new life,
and return to my comfortable room,
to my stereo and records,
to all my old customs.
But that is childish, Lord, isn't it? —
A clutching at what has been
instead of stretching out my arms
to what can be if I let it.
Yet even so,
I still feel the ache of loneliness
gnawing away inside me,
tearing me into small fragments.
Lord, be good to my parents and friends,
while I am so far beyond
the horizons of their love.

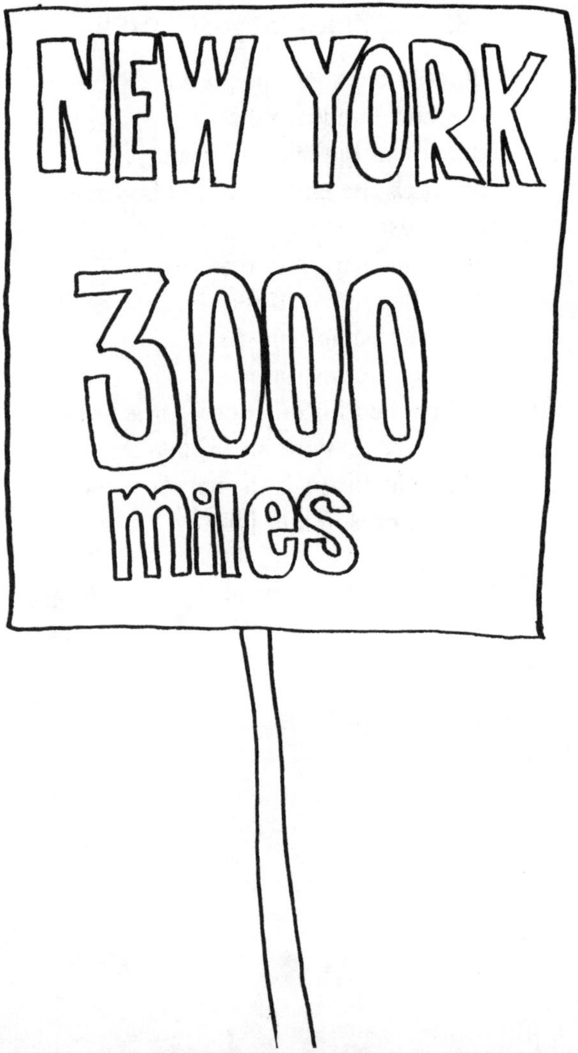
NEW YORK
3000
miles

18. PRAYER FOR A SOLDIER

Where does the time go, Lord?
It seems like just yesterday
that I was big with pregnancy,
but now the child I carried is grown,
and must be busy
about his nation's concerns.
What happened to the time
when I changed his diapers,
and tied up his shoes,
and packed his lunchbox for school,
and suffered with his broken leg,
and went through the nervousness
of his first summer job?

Where are those moments, Lord?
Gone into memories vivid as snapshots,
leaving me in this dreadful present,
ironing khaki shirts
to be worn in distant battle.
Yet this too must happen,
and become a memory,
because no one can remain a child forever.
All I ask of You, Lord,
is that You look after him over there,
as I did here,
when he moves into his hour of manhood.

19. A SOLDIER'S PRAYER

Lord, when I'm huddled
down inside the oozing mud of a ditch,
I begin to think
about what a ridiculous thing war is.
I think of myself,
who never owned a gun nor shot a rabbit,
clutching my rifle with intent to kill.
I think of my enemy,
somewhere out there
behind that scorched clump of bushes,
in the same deadly situation.
If I knew his language,
I could call to him,
saying that I really don't dislike him,
but that after all this is war,
and I want to blow his head off.
We might even laugh
about the sadness of our plight.
Yet we could never throw down our guns
and shake hands in friendship,
because at our backs
is the stiff pride of our nations,
which compels two men,
who are brothers under God,
to kill or be killed.

20. PRAYER FOR A GROOM-TO-BE

Well, Lord,
now that I've popped the fateful question
and she's responded with an energetic yes,
I just begin to realize
what deep water I've gotten myself into.
Dating was one thing,
and going steady another,
but marriage is a whole new world
in which I feel a total stranger.
Yet she does love me, Lord:
she loves my bent nose,
my shaggy eyebrows, my stubby fingers —
and even more than that,
she loves my self,
my self that I take for granted,
or get so angry with,
or on occasion could do without.
Yes, she loves me,
and her love has made me see myself
in an entirely new perspective —
through her eyes.
True, I'll have to grow some inside
before I can match her vision of me,
but, Lord, her love has given me
all the energy I'll ever need.

YES

21. PRAYER FOR THE FATHER OF THE BRIDE

She's getting married, Lord.
The awkward little girl with braces
is getting married.
I know I shouldn't feel maudlin
at a time like this,
but every minute that passes
brings her closer to leaving,
to emptying the house
of her irritating laughter,
and her reckless bounding up the stairs,
and her exasperating hours in the tub.
I suppose it's strange,
but now that she's going,
those things about her which annoyed me
are becoming precious.
Of course, I'm happy for her, Lord.
It's the most natural thing in the world
that she should grow up
and marry
and move away.
But somehow,
there's a sadness about it too,
that someone so taken for granted
could leave such a gaping hole
in the fabric of my life.

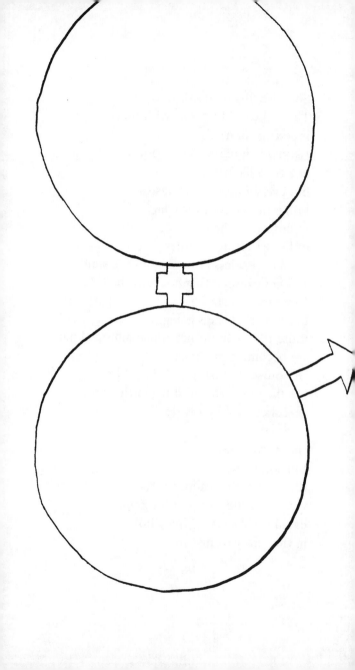

22. PRAYER ON PREGNANCY

I just got in from the doctor's, Lord,
and the tests were all positive.
Yet it's hard to believe,
because I don't feel any different.
I don't feel anything inside me
to set me apart
from the one person I was a month ago
into the two unique persons
that I am today.
Still, the poor dead rabbit
tells me for certain someone is there,
needing me,
a small strawberry of blood
that is alive and growing
and so very real.
Yet I'm frightened too, Lord,
not because of the pain to come,
but because so much can go wrong
to prevent this child from being born
or to make him be born badly.
From this time on, help us both, Lord:
myself in becoming the mother
that he needs,
and himself in becoming the human image
that You so richly deserve.

23. PRAYER ON ADOPTION

Can You hear me, Lord?
I hope so,
because I so desperately want You to.
It's just that my husband and I
want to adopt a child,
because we can't have one ourselves.
Right now, out there in the world,
women are gulping down pills
to prevent pregnancy,
and others are considering
going to an abortion mill,
because they don't want the one thing
we can't do without.
I only wish
I could get on a phone and tell them,
"Have your child,
we'll take it,
we'll take all of them,"
but that's impossible.
So instead, we put our names on lists,
and go through channels,
and fill out endless forms.
Lord, we just ask You
to give us patience
that will bear fruit before too long.

24. PRAYER ON COOKING

Lord, I admit I am no chef of the week
nor some Houdini with pots and pans,
but how could anyone be consistently
as bad at cooking as I am,
without a bit of enemy sabotage?
If I had to point a finger of blame,
I would say that my stove hates me,
because it either overcooks to a cinder
or undercooks to pure mush.
Like the cake I baked yesterday:
now I concede that bubbles on top
might be taken as sheer artistry,
and the sagging middle I could patent,
but why did it taste like sweet grit?
So what do I do now? —
The stove is too new to dip in bronze
for preserving as a memento,
and the idea of living on raw food
is too radical to take seriously.
Yet something must happen soon, Lord,
since my husband can hardly survive
on a daily diet of Pop-Tarts.
I'm willing to capitulate for improvement,
if only You can persuade my stove
to be a friend, at least part time.

BLESS US, O LORD

25. PRAYER FOR MEALTIME

Once again, Lord,
we will be sitting down together
to a common meal of common food:
some meat, some milk,
some vegetables, some bread.
Yet this is also an uncommon meal,
because each item before us
has been prepared with special love,
and each bite will be eaten among friends.
Who can ever say
which is more important, Lord:
the food that nourishes our bodies,
or the friendship that feeds our souls?
It is true that all the world over
men are craving both of these blessings,
and yet we take them for granted.
Help us, Lord,
to become strong at this table,
strong in both body and soul,
so that we might rise up better people,
who can go forth to the world
and feed its starving,
no matter in what guise
this hunger might appear.
Amen.

26. PRAYER ON RELAXATION

Lately, Lord,
I've been running around in circles,
doing things and buying things,
so that right now
I'm just about panting with exhaustion.
Every week I promise
to take time out for myself,
but I never do it,
because it looks like such a luxury.
I don't know why it is
but I seem to equate work with virtue,
and relaxation with vice.
Maybe it's my Puritan heritage
riding around inside my conscience;
but the point is I must resist it.
I need to replenish myself
before the well runs dry,
before I work myself to death.
Most especially,
I must become aware of my own value.
I do things for others,
but right now
it's time to do something for myself.
Lord, let me remember this resolve
from time to time.

This is the time

27. PRAYER ON HOUSECLEANING

Sometimes, Lord, I wonder
why I don't wrap my entire house
in a plastic garbage bag
and throw it out with the trash.
In the long run
it would be simpler than the ritual
of raking dirt from the rugs,
or scooping dust from the chairs,
or polishing the tarnish
from my set of dime-store utensils.
Still, I guess the problem's mine alone,
at least in this household, Lord,
because my husband wouldn't mind
walking around on grit floors
or sleeping on a gunny sack,
just as my son wouldn't mind
wearing pants of multicolor mud.
Somehow, this repulsion by filth
must come from my soul's precision
which demands order and cleanliness
everywhere it looks.
Well, Lord,
if that's my notion of salvation,
at least give me the stamina to gain it,
for what it might be worth in Your eyes.

28. PRAYER ON JURY DUTY

I've been called up for jury duty, Lord,
and it has really gotten me nervous.
When the notice arrived, I thought,
"Surely, there must be some mistake";
and then later on,
"But I can't give up all that time";
and finally I panicked into thinking,
"Who do I know to get me out of it?"
It's not being in the court of justice
that has thrown me, Lord;
not the ponderous machinery of law,
nor the solemnity of the occasion,
nor being with eleven total strangers.
What's gotten to me,
that won't even let me sleep or eat,
is the fact of passing judgment:
me, with my grade-school intellect
and my single secret vote,
deciding on the guilt or innocence
of some unique human being.
With much hesitation and misgivings,
I intend to perform my duty, Lord,
but please be with me in that jury box,
because the responsibility I carry
is weighing me down.

fly the
friendly skies

29. PRAYER FOR JET FLIGHT

You remember me, Lord:
I'm the fidgety one
that's scared to death of heights;
that same one that's now strapped
so tightly into this plane seat
that my legs are turning purple.
I've never flown before, Lord,
so You'd do me a great favor
if You'd give this bus with wings
Your undivided attention.
I've read novels about jets,
so I know what can go wrong with them:
the tail could blow off,
the engines could overheat,
some crackpot could have stored a bomb
in any piece of innocuous luggage,
or one of my fellow jet setters
could get a hankering to visit Cuba.
It's not that I'm panicking;
I've done that long ago.
It's just that I tend to worry
about the other passengers.
How do You think they'll feel, Lord,
if I have to be carried off this flight
in a total collapse?

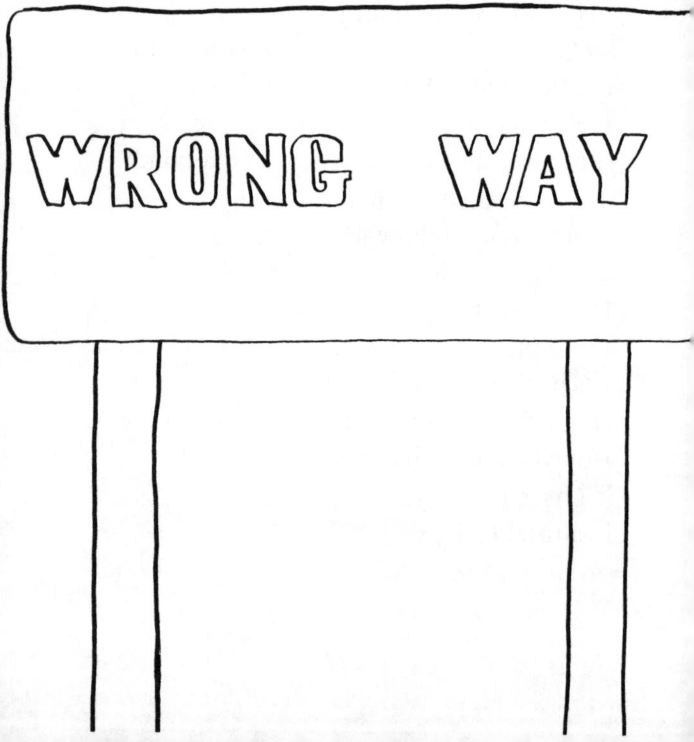
WRONG WAY

30. PRAYER FOR BAD MORNINGS

Well, Lord,
I certainly got off
to a running start this morning.
Already I've overslept my alarm,
bruised my leg against a chair
while rushing to get dressed,
burned my tongue
gulping down coffee hot as lava,
and I managed to pick fights
with the whole family during breakfast.

If I don't watch myself,
I'll develop a bad case
of the 24-hour uglies
which proves contagious to all I meet.
So, Lord, I'm asking You
to shine some sun on the rest of the day,
not just for me alone,
but for those I come in contact with,
especially my own family.
They deserve more than putting up
with a rain cloud in the living room.
I've already killed the morning
by letting my surly temper loose:
now help me to smile
upon this day's remaining moments.

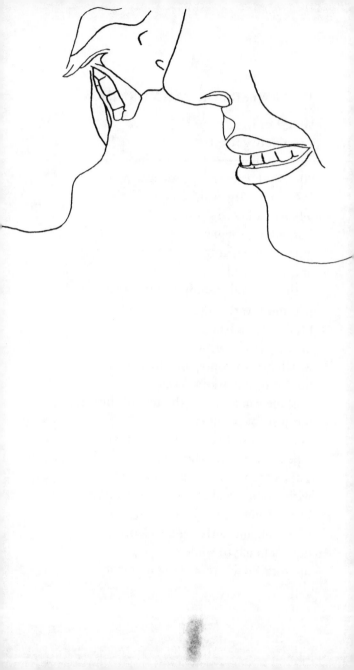

31. PRAYER ON MARRIAGE

The other day, Lord,
when I was cleaning out the closet,
I found our album of wedding pictures.
I paged through it slowly,
remembering the vows,
the ring ceremony,
the hail of rice,
the cutting of the cake;
remembering so many things
that I had forgotten for years.
What struck me most about the snapshots
was the smiles and the joy,
page after page of happiness,
captured in black and white for all time.
And now where is it,
when the same people of the photographs
argue heatedly over money,
slam doors in anger,
or shout from room to room?
Gone with the wind, I guess.
But does it have to remain so?
Lord, help me to put
some of the tenderness and love
back into our marriage,
but mainly help me put back the smiles.

32. PRAYER ON APPLE PICKING

Yesterday, Lord,
as my husband and I were driving home
from visiting friends in the country,
we saw one of those road signs
which read,
"Pick all the apples you want,"
and it named a price.
Well, since we're city dwellers,
we decided to take the farmer up on it.
The day was crisp,
with a ceiling of leaves over us
just beginning to yellow at the edges,
and we were the only ones around
with our empty bushelbaskets.
To be honest,
the last thing that we needed
was a trunkload of apples,
but we picked them
until our arches ached from climbing,
and our arms were sore from reaching,
just for the pleasure
of doing something different.
Today we're back to normal, Lord,
but those few golden hours
will stay with me forever.

33. PRAYER ON COLDS

Well, Lord, go ahead and congratulate me
for being the prize idiot I am,
because now I have a perfect case
of the common cold,
and I either got it
by raking the front lawn
in my skimpy sweat shirt,
or by sitting for three frozen hours
at a tragic football game.
Yet don't blame me too loudly, Lord,
because my suffering now
must surely expiate my foolishness.
Just look at me:
my head feels like a balloon
filled with jelly,
my nose is running like a faucet,
and all I can do is wheeze
between gasps for breath.
All right, Lord, You've made Your point
that I'm not blessed
with the health of Tarzan,
nor his climate,
and that I should take more precautions.
Now, just help me get over this cold
so I can put Your wisdom into practice.

34. PRAYER FOR WINTER

It's snowing our first snow, Lord,
with flakes the size of soap bubbles
floating past the window.
I've got the heat turned up
and I'm in my wool sweater,
so I don't feel the cold,
but out there it's dropping fast.
The winter change is on us,
the slow closing down of nature's world,
turning everything indoors.
These dark days
are perfectly shaped for thinking,
for sitting down
over a cup of hot chocolate
and stirring my problems into order.
At least, Lord,
that's how I think of winter,
as a period of hibernation
and introspection,
so that when the last snowflake
vanishes from the ground
and the spring thaw
knocks at the sleeping roots,
I'll be ready with the rest of the world
to rise and start anew.

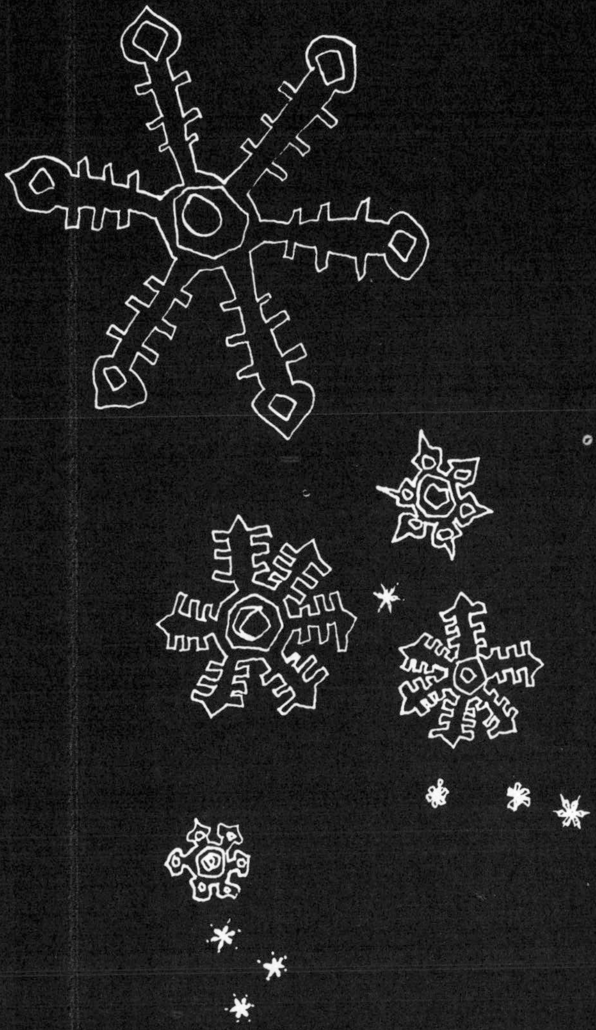

35. PRAYER ON RELATIVES

This afternoon, Lord, I must begin
my annual round of visiting relatives,
checking them off as I go
so that I don't slight any.
Visiting friends is pleasant, Lord,
it's relaxing, it's renewing;
but visiting relatives
who are little more than strangers
is an obligation that you're born with
or marry into,
which usually ends up being nothing
but a drain on the nervous system.

They show you their cat
which hates you instantly,
or their nervous canary
which turns sullen and refuses to sing;
they take you down to the cellar
to inspect their damson preserves,
or upstairs to view the attic;
they show you the fine points of sewing.
All I ask, Lord, is the grace
to sit through it without yawning,
because my slim once-a-year visit
may mean more to them
than I'll ever know.

36. PRAYER FOR FEBRUARY

Well, Lord, it's February,
the in-between month,
filled neither with January's cold
nor March's wind,
and I sit here at the window
as in-between as the month,
wondering how long the snowman
will last on my melting front lawn.
There are things I should be doing,
like the dishes or the wash,
but I feel so listless, Lord,
like a damp rag left in the sink.
I could always flick on the TV
and pass a dull hour
viewing commercialized boredom,
but the melodrama of the soap operas
doesn't come on till later,
so even that's out of the question.
Lord, all I ask
is that You help me get through
this in-between time of the year
and of my life,
and back into the center of things,
because this way I'm no use to anyone,
not even myself.

37. PRAYER FOR GOOD SAMARITANS

Well, Lord, I don't suppose
You ever had a flat tire in midwinter,
when the roads are deep slush,
and the snow keeps slashing at you
in sharp nuggets of ice.
Believe me, it's an experience,
especially when you open the car trunk
and are surprised to find a jack
that doesn't look strong enough
to lift a toy wagon,
let alone two tons of bulky machinery.
Yet it wasn't something all bad,
because through it I learned
that people can be generous,
even despite their own discomfort.
I learned this when a truck driver —
whose name I can't even remember —
stopped to lend a hand,
and when a young girl pulled over
to ask if there had been an accident.
It made me feel good inside, Lord,
to discover that there are still
good samaritans in the world,
who could care enough for an unknown man
to offer free and spontaneous help.

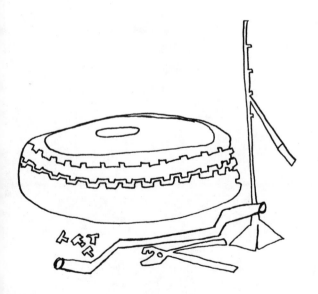

38. PRAYER FOR AN OLD CAR

Well, Lord,
I think my four-wheeled yacht
is about ready to roll over and die,
because all I get from her is a wheeze,
accompanied by a cacophony of knocks
that sounds like bad plumbing.
Still I must admit she served me well,
and deserves a decent burial
in the graveyard of defunct cars.
Who knows,
I may even shed a tear or two,
although sympathy
for a heap of gears and spark plugs
isn't popular these days.
And why not?
She certainly had spirit.
She pulled me to safety
away from many a driver's recklessness;
she carried my family
from mountain snow to ocean salt.
Now she's dying,
another victim of planned obsolescence.
May she rust quietly, Lord,
while I go scouting for a newer model
that will never quite take her place.

39. A DRIVER'S PRAYER

Taking the car out on the highway
is no pleasure any more, Lord.
It's an awful responsibility,
threading a ton of rushing machinery
through a maze of obstacles
to reach a necessary destination.
Anything could happen,
any other driver could act recklessly,
even I could miscalculate
and send myself and those with me
hurtling to a speedy death.
Yet I must venture out on the road:
I have places to get to, Lord,
appointments to keep,
people to ferry back and forth.
I don't want to blow this
out of proportion,
but I could honestly use Your help.
I know I have the skill,
but sometimes
even that isn't enough.
So, Lord,
be with me as a fellow traveler
when I'm out there
in the world of trucks and cars.

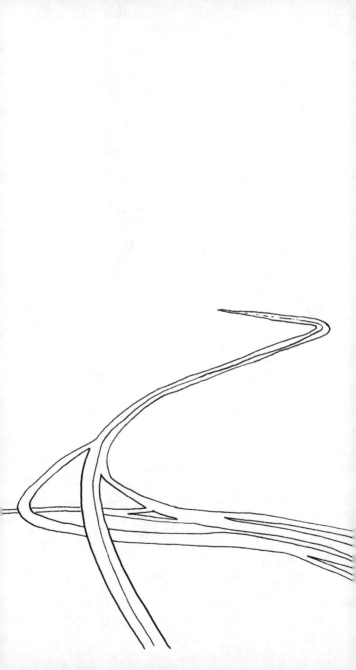

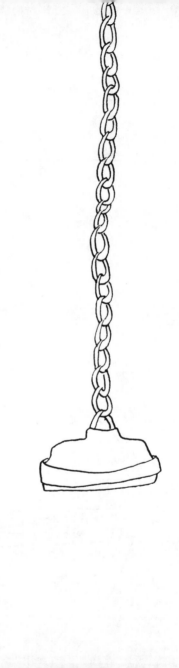

40. PRAYER ON BLOOD

I cut my finger with my razor
while shaving this morning, Lord,
and didn't think much of it
until I rinsed off the blood.
It swirled around in a whirlpool
of frothy lather and water,
then disappeared down the drain
with the other sewage.

Then I thought:
what an ugly end
to something that was part of myself,
that had a life of its own
as it swam blindly
through the channels of my veins.
I wasn't trying to be morbid, Lord,
but it seemed strange
to see it go without rites of burial —
those tiny cells of blood
that had looked after me,
serviced me selflessly,
kept me fit for the contest of living.
Lord, let me become better aware
of the reverence I owe my body
because within it are more secret lives
than I'll ever know.

41. A DOCTOR'S PRAYER

I'm proud of my profession, Lord,
if only people didn't expect so much.
The truth of the matter is
many lavish me with awe
that would more befit a pagan deity.
If they have a weight problem,
or a racking cough,
or even an ingrown toenail,
then see me — all will be well.
Yet it's not these minor quirks
of a distempered nature
that get inside me and fester,
but rather the great ones, Lord —
when they sit in the outer office
with bovine eyes of trust
and expect the customary miracle.
It's times like that when this deity
must show his feet of clay
and plead utter helplessness;
for You alone, Lord,
possess the power of life and death.
And not until people admit this
can my profession and myself
stand on our own scientific ground
without the trappings of mummery.

42. PRAYER ON PHYSICAL FITNESS

Lord, I suspect
if I wanted to keep America beautiful
I would have to begin with me.
When I was younger,
I rushed around everywhere,
burned up calories by the carload,
and stayed trim without effort.
But now I'm a more sedentary creature:
I ride instead of walk,
I sit instead of stand,
I relax by watching others
instead of letting them watch me.
Naturally I have gained an ounce or two,
have developed several bulges,
and have a hard time finding clothes
which both fit and are attractive.
I suppose
I should do something about it:
I should diet or exercise,
or maybe even both.
But that will take an effort, Lord,
so I'm asking You to give me
a little push in my personal campaign
to beautify America
by beautifying myself.

KEEP AMERICA BEAUTIFUL ★ ★ ★

43. A POSTMAN'S PRAYER

I've been at this job 10 years, Lord,
walking how many thousands of miles,
stopping at how many millions of doors,
delivering how many
innumerable pieces of mail.
At first, I noticed nothing
but my bone tiredness as day dragged on,
and the ache in my arches,
and the cramp in my back.
But lately, Lord,
I've become aware of something else:

the priceless cargo of letters
that I carry along —
because behind each one is a story.
In this brown envelope
is a government check for an old man;
in that one, of pale pink,
the bubbling sentences of a teenager;
in this smudged one,
the heroic words of a soldier overseas;
in that of rich white,
the joyful announcement of marriage.
Lord, my task is small,
but thank You for the privilege
of serving the wonderful race of man.

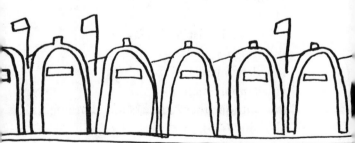

44. PRAYER ON LONELINESS

I feel so isolated from everyone, Lord,
the way Adam felt in the garden
before You gave him Eve.
I S O L A T E D . . .
the word sounds like an iceberg
lost in an infinite ocean of silence.
I know I shouldn't feel this way,
that I have many friends
only a phone call away,
that You at least are here.

But I still feel it gnawing at me.
This dark mood will pass —
it always does —
but right now I'm trapped in it,
so I might as well put it to use.
After all,
it's probably just Your way
of letting me know
how dependent I am on others
who support me,
how without them I'm less than nothing.
All right, Lord,
I thank You for this insight,
but now,
please help me to stop feeling blue.

45. A SMOKER'S PRAYER

Why do I do it, Lord?
I haven't the slightest idea any more.
In the beginning,
there was a certain pleasure to it,
a slow release of tension,
a moment's peace.
But now, nothing:
nothing but a bad taste in my mouth,
a fuzzy tongue,
and lungs as black as a coal mine.
So why do I do it?
Probably just out of habit,
a reaching for something
that once had meaning,
hoping the meaning will return.
Yet what good is a crutch
that doesn't support,
that bends like rubber with use?
No good, I suppose,
especially when I'm forced
to spend more on it every year.
So, Lord, help me
to feel how stupid the habit is,
and then maybe I'll develop sense
someday soon.

46. PRAYER FOR A COMMON MAN

Sometimes I sit here, Lord,
watching TV,
when a juggling act comes on,
or a singing group,
or a movie with a crowd scene —
and suddenly I notice some little person.
Usually he's not in the spotlight,
nor the one singing solo,
nor the character with the speaking part.
Rather, he's the one who's just there,
holding a prop,
or humming in the background,
or depositing cash as the bank is robbed.

And then I think,
watch over that person, Lord,
whoever he might be,
because he's so much like me,
small, unobtrusive, unnoticed,
but still necessary
for whatever successes
the spotlight people might achieve.
We're not much, Lord,
but we do serve a purpose,
like duller threads
on the vast loom of Your plan.

47. A STRIKER'S PRAYER

I never thought it might happen, Lord,
but the vote carried by a majority,
so now we are committed to striking.
I believe that, morally,
we are doing the right thing,
because my old wages couldn't purchase
what they would five years back.
But still, until the new raise comes in,
we tighten our belts and suffer.
My girls can't go to parties,
my wife can't get that new winter coat,
we buy brand-X groceries,
and I am forced to live without tobacco.
Since all of us
are involved in this thing, Lord,
hurry the end of negotiations,
because they could drag on for months,
and then where are we?
Of course, I know
there are more important issues at stake
than the personal comfort of my family.
But, Lord,
they are closer to me
than any abstract principle,
so I just can't help feeling concerned.

48. A POLICEMAN'S PRAYER

Lately, Lord,
I almost hate to get up in the morning,
to put on my uniform and badge,
to face the ordeal of duty.
Will I have to meet
a barrage of abusive language?
Will I be forced to billy club
some anonymous person in a riot?
Will I stand in cross-haired focus
before a rooftop sniper?
I pray not, Lord,
but if it happens, be with me,
because if I give up,
I submit to the lawlessness
I once promised to combat,
to the crime
I once swore to prohibit,
to the violence
I once vowed to root out.
I know my duty, Lord,
and I will live it
to the fullest extent of my capability.
But You must be with me too,
since my failure will mean much more
than just personal defeat.

WHITE
BLACK
LIVE
TOGETHER

49 PRAYER ON INTEGRATION

Well, Lord, they've finally done it,
broken into a block of homes
that stood for years on end
as an impregnable bastion of whiteness.
The outcome was predictable,
even when first we banded together
in secret pact to prevent just this.
Were we selfish, Lord,
to want the old values and neighborhood
to remain unchanged forever?
Or were we just prejudiced,
demanding that our eyes behold
only an arbitrary skin pigmentation?
Or, maybe, were we plain scared,
frightened that land prices would drop,
that no one would be safe after dark?
I don't know, I honestly don't know.
But what difference does it make
now that the black change is upon us?
Today, Lord, all I can ask of You
is the grace to see this moment
through their glad eyes of rejoicing,
because while for me an ideal is dying,
for them, in their stoical patience,
an ideal has finally been achieved.

50. PRAYER ON POLLUTION

When I was younger, Lord,
there was a small woodland acre
just a few feet from our back door,
with a little brook bubbling through it,
so clear I could drink its waters.
But now, in its place,
there is an apartment building
where children play at sailing boats
down slimy cement gutters,
and nearby, a few stunted trees
too sick to grow into great ones.
I know that people must live somewhere,
and I respect this need, Lord,
but must they make all things ugly
by their presence?
Even now we have nothing
but litter in the streets,
and scum on the rivers,
and soot in the air,
and oil slicks on the lakes and oceans.
If the world is made in Your image, Lord,
I wonder how future generations
will think of You,
when the earth has finally become
a vast rubble of garbage.

51. PRAYER ON PEST CONTROL

I hate to admit it, Lord,
but I have roaches:
shiny red ones that lurk
near that damp spot in the cellar.
So what do I do now?
Already I've looked for advice
in a fat handbook on insects;
but it said nothing
except that they were approximately
as old as the dinosaur.
Obviously, they must have staying power,
if they've outwitted
man's exterminating instincts this long.
In all honesty,
they haven't been obnoxious tenants yet,
but I still feel we're incompatible.
All those legs and antennae get to me.
I suppose
I'll have to murder them with a spray,
or with those pellets
that disappear in the night,
leaving nothing but corpses behind.
In any case, Lord,
I thank You for Your pets,
though they were hardly what I expected.

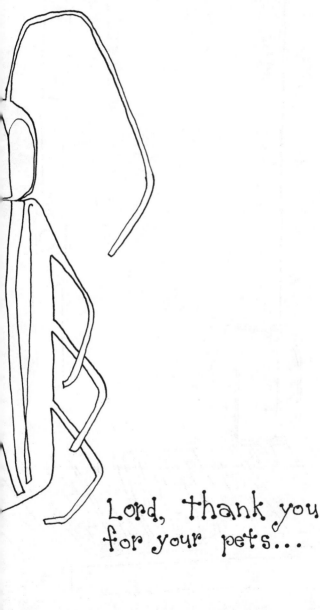

Lord, thank you
for your pets...

52. PRAYER ON A NEW HOME

Well, Lord, we're finally moving
from our sardine can of an apartment,
where the sink dripped,
and the plaster fell off in hunks,
and the wind whistled
in eerie tones through the windows.
From now on,
look for us in the suburbs,
in a canary-yellow cottage
with a thick lawn out front,
and a large yard out back,
and a WELCOME sign
on the mat before the door.
Yet don't think it was luxury alone
that attracted us, Lord,
because it was more than that:
it was our wanting elbowroom
after city cramp;
of safe streets
after ominous alleys;
of decent schools
after cardboard classrooms.
Please, Lord, help us
to reach a watershed of happiness now,
after years of purgatory in the city.

53. PRAYER ON GOING HOME

I've been away for years, Lord,
but the other day
I managed to drive back home,
to the same town where I was born,
to the same streets where I played,
to the same house
where I grew up with my family.
In my most pleasant daydreams
I often went back there,
walking under the gnarled oak trees
to the piping of birds,
passing blueberry pies cooling in windows,
seeing the faces of my friends.
Reality was harsher, Lord,
because the town had changed
into a sullen village
of prefab houses and supermarkets,
with my own home a loan office.
Not one friend was left,
except those that had stayed behind
in the graveyard.
Maybe it was good, Lord,
to have my dream shattered forever,
because now I realize
that no one can go back home again.

54. PRAYER ON A DEAD HOUSE

Two streets down, Lord,
in the middle of the block,
there's a dead house.
I say *dead,*
because it's more than just vacant:
it's gutted,
with windows broken,
and ceilings fallen away,
and leaves piling in the corners.
It makes me sad to see it, Lord,
because just a few years back
there were voices booming in its rooms;
there were young children
peering from the doorway;
there was life in every inch of it.
But somehow, things change,
people move away,
and death settles quietly in the rubble.
I'm not usually emotional, Lord,
yet it's hard not to think of how,
some distant day,
my own home will be like that:
a hollow shell,
emptied of all the memories
that I now hold so precious.

55. PRAYER ON TRADITION

I saw the balloon man today, Lord,
the same one who came with his box
of multicolored, multishaped balloons
every Saturday when I was young,
who filled them
with his compressor of helium
right to the point of bursting;
so many of them
they seemed about to carry him
from the earth.
Today, Lord, when I saw him,
I saw nothing but a sad little man,
shrunken up with age,
and shorn of the magic
that once lured children to him.
I don't know why,
but it made me think of our traditions
enshrined like jewels in our feelings,
so rare and so beautiful,
but now nothing
but paste and imitation glitter.
It depresses me, Lord,
to realize that even traditions
shrivel up and grow outdated
like the balloon man.

56. PRAYER FOR A DEAD FRIEND

I feel strange, Lord,
because while I was sitting here
quietly reading the papers,
someone very close to me
was lying in an antiseptic room
dying.
I didn't even know
that part of me was being cut off,
the precious part which was my friend,
so that now just half of me is alive,
and the other half
has slipped away into Your care.
And what can I do?
Heal myself, I guess:
close over the gaping wound of separation
and prepare for a new start.
Yet that's not all:
I only now begin to realize
that my friend still lives in me,
in my memory,
in my feelings.
I must keep these feelings alive,
because if I don't,
then something beautiful
will truly have vanished from the earth.

57. PRAYER ON YESTERDAY

Lord, what ever happened
to the good old days?
I don't know,
but I feel so far away
from the golden time of my childhood,
from picking berries in the hot sun,
or catching crawfish in the creek,
or walking down a country lane
where the only sound you heard
was the buzz of bees.
Those times are gone, Lord,
gone for good in this age of machinery
and computerized stoplights
and buildings that stretch
from here to the North Star.
I know it's best to be positive,
to dwell on what's gained for mankind
instead of on what's lost.
But Lord, that's hard to do,
especially when you think of the young
growing up in these cement canyons,
looking back to now
from some future date,
and wistfully remembering these
as the good old days.

58. PRAYER ON THE MENTALLY ILL

Last night, Lord,
I was paging through an old magazine
when I came across a picture article
on the mentally ill.
It shook me, because their eyes
seemed to burn with fierce fever
as they stared out of the photographs,
and I couldn't help wondering
what they saw:
the same commonplace world
of tables and chairs which I see,
or some fantastic nightmare garden
which only twisted souls could journey.
What a terrible waste, Lord,
because they are healthy
in every way but mind.
Yet they bother me too,
since they were once sane as myself,
but now I am here in normal society,
while they are locked away
until their mental night can be lighted.
Help me, Lord,
to get over my aversion of them,
because they are nothing but myself,
except for Your mysterious grace.

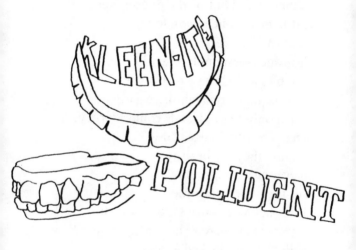

59. PRAYER ON FALSE TEETH

Lord, I'm married to a clacker
whose false teeth fit so poorly
that you'd think his mouth
was filled with castanets.
Now, that type of thing
might be fine for flamenco music,
but it does grate on the nerves
as a breakfast serenade.
Naturally, he's sensitive about it,
and although it's driving me
to digging my nails in the wall,
I will remain steadfast to silence.
Still, this doesn't exclude subtle hints,
like opening the newspaper
to ads on those pastes and powders
intended for just this problem.
As a senior citizen, Lord,
I can't otherwise complain:
we own our home,
we have no outstanding debts;
he has his poker; I have my bingo.
Life's almost perfect, Lord,
and it will be,
after You and I team up
to solve this last great trial.

60. PRAYER ON SENILITY

My mother is old, Lord,
and, naturally,
is getting a bit fuzzy in her mind.
Well, my great problem
is in having patience with her,
especially when she does strange things.
Like the time
she hid her false teeth in the freezer,
or spoon-fed whiskey to our cat
because it looked tired,
or dropped a fork
down the garbage disposal
as an experiment.
I do admit that these things
have their funny side to them,
but, Lord,
I remember my mother a different way,
and it tears me up inside.
How can I dare be harsh with her
when I recall
how she nursed me through fever,
or calmed me the morning of my marriage,
or taught me that love means sacrifice?
Help me remember this last lesson, Lord,
when my patience wears thin.

GIVE ME PATIENCE, LORD

61. PRAYER FOR THE SICK

I hurt again, Lord,
I hurt all over.
From the very onset of my sickness,
I rebelled against pain,
I hid behind my medicine bottles,
I threw myself at You
in what must have been pure melodrama,
begging a reprieve.
Yet somehow You must have seen
something valuable about pain
because it's still here.
I suppose I should be thankful,
but I'm not very heroic.
I can't smile with gratitude
when my body is on the torture rack.
All I ask, Lord,
is that You help me grasp
the worth of the hurt twisting inside me,
because if I knew that,
maybe I'd be able to bear up better,
maybe then I wouldn't be so cranky
with those I love most.
But no matter what, Lord,
just help me get through today
without being too much of a burden.

62. PRAYER ON PILLS

Lately, Lord,
I've been wondering what cavemen did
when they had a headache,
vitamin deficiency, or iron-poor blood.
Obviously, they didn't run
to their Stone-age medicine cabinets
for some new miracle drug,
so they must have gritted their teeth
and suffered through it unaided.
In this age, that is unbelievable.
If we have a pain, Lord,
we just gulp three green disks
or one red capsule
and we're set for another day.
Yet the medicine show has me worried:
there are too many unknown side effects
for us to continue throwing pills
recklessly down our throats.
Maybe in the long run,
it's better to endure a minor ache
than to ruin the whole bodily system
with a cure that missed its mark.
Lord, let me remember this
the next time some TV healer
comes on with his pitch.

63. PRAYER FOR AUTUMN

It's autumn, Lord,
the time when sunlight slants strangely
through the yellow prisms of the trees,
and leaves twirl down
like butterflies dancing.
It makes me feel melancholy, Lord,
to think of the year
getting decked out in bright colors
for a final fling before winter.
Something like myself, I suppose,
dyeing the hair a shade darker
and rubbing some warmth on the cheeks
before admitting
that I'm too old for the game.

Yet, that's the way we all go, Lord,
kicking up our heels in spring,
becoming fruitful in summer,
moving slowly
through the halfway house of autumn
before our age catches up with us
and winter settles in.
It was a good year, Lord,
and a good life,
and I only ask for the wisdom
to let us both go out with grace.

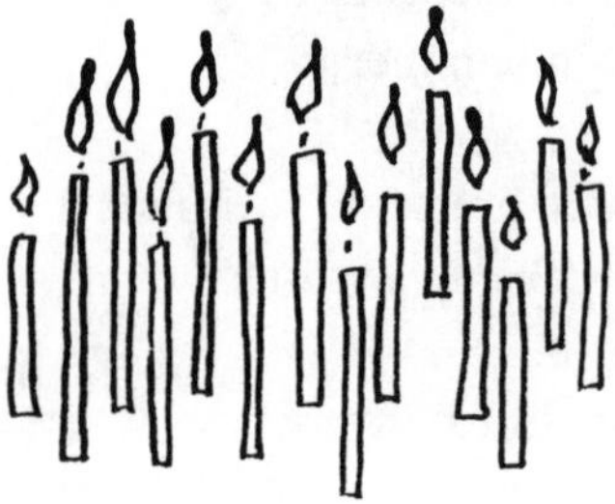

64. A BIRTHDAY PRAYER

Today, Lord,
for what it might be worth,
is the anniversary
of my entering into the world.
As on every past birthday,
there will be a small celebration
within the family circle;
there will be the table high with gifts;
there will be the blowing out of candles
on the minuscule cake.
But still, when I stare in the mirror
at the creases on my aging face,
I wonder whether this yearly ritual
means anything.
After all, I've done nothing
but the usual things in a usual way,
and any of a million men
could have taken my place in line
with little difference.
Yet my birth must mean something, Lord,
or else You would have never let me be.
Today, before it is too late,
help me discover my own special worth
so that I might spend it joyfully
all of my remaining years.

65. PRAYER ON GROWING OLD

Lord, it's difficult to admit
that I'm not as young as I once was,
although aging is a natural process
which all men must face.
It's not so much the being old
that is difficult to bear,
not the sagging wrinkles,
the false teeth,
the heavy underclothing in winter,
but rather it's the obsolescence,
the growing out of date and unimportant
that is the agony.
When you are young,
you thrash about with vital energy
trying to make your mark on the world,
but when you are old
you are forced by your own tired body
to sit quietly by
watching as others move up
to write over what you have written,
or erase it altogether.
Let me be wise in my growing old, Lord,
knowing that I have done what I could,
and smiling with peace as another
takes his turn in the game of life.

AMERICAN CANCER SOCIETY

66. PRAYER ON CANCER

What's the matter with me, Lord?
All I know
is that I have this pain
gnawing away at me constantly,
so constantly
I don't think I can bear it much longer.
I had an operation last year, Lord,
and the doctor said it was a success,
with no trace of malignancy.
Yet this pain
makes me fear he was withholding,
that there is something there,
some cancerous growth
crawling within me.
If I have to die, Lord, I'm ready.
But let me die quickly,
not the slow death of cancer,
which begins in sedation
and ends with a skinny skeleton of bones
while the parasite
feeds inside its victim.
In any case, Lord, help me;
help me to survive the pain,
and the doctor's new sentence,
whatever it might be.

67. PRAYER FOR A DEAD HUSBAND

Now that I've pulled myself together
after my initial bout with tears,
I think I'll be all right, Lord,
more capable of thinking
about my husband and his passing
without going into deep shock again.
He is dead, Lord,
laid out in that blue suit of his
we picked up at the half-price sale,
wearing the striped tie
I gave him for a present last Christmas.
Yet I've never seen him look so formal;
not even asleep did he look this way;
so stern you'd think he was angry.
No matter, for I have my memories, Lord,
of the way he looked when we first met,
how his face crinkled up in laughter,
how his eyes gleamed behind his glasses.
He was a good man,
as good a man as ever I could want.
But now he's gone,
leaving this strange shell behind.
Be gentle with him, Lord,
and let him remember me too,
from time to time.

68. PRAYER FOR THE OLD

When I sit here at night, Lord,
I get to thinking
that my world is peopled by no one
but the dead.
Just look at my Christmas mailing list:
one name scratched out after another,
till I can cover my remaining friends
with a handful of cards.
And even then one of those comes back
with *DECEASED*
stamped in black letters across it.

Another one gone,
with myself as the last survivor
of a vanished age
of frail lace dresses,
and delicate lorgnettes,
and pink lemonade at the summer pavilion.
It's no wonder
I ask to be left alone with my memories,
instead of poked at by doctors' tools
or looked after by kindly neighbors.
I'm the last one, Lord,
the last leaf on a dead tree,
counting my days
till I'm with my friends again.

69. PRAYER FOR A WAKE

This afternoon, Lord,
I have to go out to a wake,
and I hate thinking about it,
not so much because a friend is gone,
but because of what
they'll have done to change him.
He was manly, Lord,
with hands like sledge hammers;
but they'll have him laid out
in a tailored suit,
when all I saw him wear was overalls;
in a funeral barge
fit for an Egyptian Pharaoh,
when he would have picked a cedar box
because of its raw strength;
and made up beyond all recognition,
when a three-days' growth of beard
was more typical.
My only consolation, Lord,
is that he won't have to be there
to witness himself in splendor,
but will have already slipped away
from this grotesque masquerade of homage.
If Jesus is yet a carpenter's Son, Lord,
he'll be happy.

70. PRAYER FOR A SUNNY DAY

Today is a good day, Lord,
with thick buttery sunlight
spread around everywhere,
and I feel like Easter all over.
I think I'm going to laugh a lot today,
because I'm so happy, Lord,
that I can't keep the lid down
on the bright emotions bubbling in me.
Even little things
which I didn't notice yesterday
have become large and important
in the yellow grace of the sun,
things like the sparkle on the cups
and the rainbow in a drop of water.
Lord, Your world is just too beautiful
to be endured for long.
I know that there are people
dying somewhere today, Lord,
in a quiet corner of agony,
but this day makes me feel
there must be something good about death,
something I never saw before.
Lord, on dismal mornings,
let me remember today
and the things I feel.

71. PRAYER ON MODERN WAR

Every nation has had its soldiers, Lord,
its gladiators in the arena,
and our nation is no different.
Yet in a special way,
the war they wage is unlike other wars
because it is called a battle of ideas,
ideas such as liberty versus bondage,
of democracy versus communism,
of the open state versus the closed one.
Still, it is men that must die
that ideas might win.
I wonder how many men, Lord,
know what ideas they are battling for
and represent,
like so many expendable pawns
on the chessboard of the world
where leaders maneuver for checkmate.
Aren't there less costly ways to victory,
even a victory of one idea over another,
than blood, bombs, and death?
If there are, Lord,
let us find them quickly
before nothing remains of the earth
but the holocaust of two ideas
exploding.

72. PRAYER FOR AN UNKNOWN CHILD

At this moment, Lord, somewhere,
a child is letting out
his first scream of existence.
Most likely I don't know his parents,
and probably I will never meet him,
but does that prevent me
from wishing him well?
Perhaps he is even being born
in some nation enemy to mine,
but does that make him
my enemy at this moment,
even if later he will aim his bullets
at the best men my country has bred?
At this moment, Lord,
before he has become part of any ideology,
I love that child in all his innocence,
the child that I too once was,
before education, before bias.
Despite all the artificial boundaries
which exist between us,
I pray him grace, Lord,
the grace You bestow upon us so freely,
that of meeting You
and of responding,
as I pray I have.

73. PRAYER ON A PENCIL

I was just sitting here, Lord,
doodling with my pencil,
when it struck me as something strange.
Here was a sharpened lead pencil,
common to me since kindergarten,
yet odd at the same time.
It was graphite from Pennsylvania,
timber from Oregon,
rubber from Brazil,
all stamped together in one instrument
intended for my personal use.
It was all those people
in all those places —
down in coal mines,
high up in mountains,
deep in steaming jungles,
digging, cutting, tapping —
striving together for my comfort,
so I could doodle and scratch sentences.
Lord, if so many separate human beings
can work together to produce something
so slight as a pencil,
why can't we work together
to create something more significant,
like universal love or world peace?

74. PRAYER ON SPACE TRAVEL

What's out there, Lord,
among those sputtering stars
that glitter
like diamonds on black velvet?
I ask because I have an ache to know.
Before man had set foot
on the dusty face of the moon,
I thought that the answer
would slip through our fingers always,
and so was content with ignorance.
But now the answer looms ahead of us:
the journey is planned,
the dates are set,
the stars will be ours forever.
Yet they will never be mine,
because I'm just too old
and earthbound
to swim in a sea light-years away,
or watch the stars from a new viewpoint,
or one day walk the grassy meadows
of another planet.
For me, the journey is closed, Lord,
but there are my children.
For them let me dream,
and so rest satisfied.

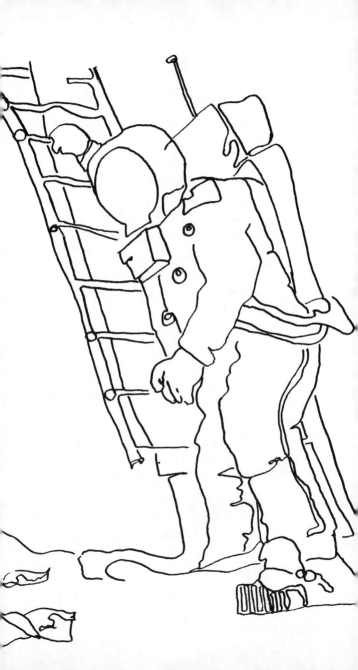

75. A CITIZEN'S PRAYER

I love America, Lord,
love her as much as I love myself.
Yet she is nothing but an abstraction,
the sum of all her people
and all their dreams,
solidified into one massive landscape.
It is our dreams which make America,
the little visions of little people
multiplied how many million times
until they overwhelm with greatness,
a monumental hope
which pushes the seas apart
as it rushes upward.
But these are troubled times, Lord,
times of suspicion and mistrust,
times of fear and doubt,
when the dreams have broken apart
in separate visions and isolated hopes.
We need You again, Lord,
as much as when we first became
one nation under God;
help us, now and forever,
to merge those dreams together once more
in the single melting pot
which is America.